J976.3 LaDo

LaDoux, Rita, 1951-

Louisiana /

LOUISIANA

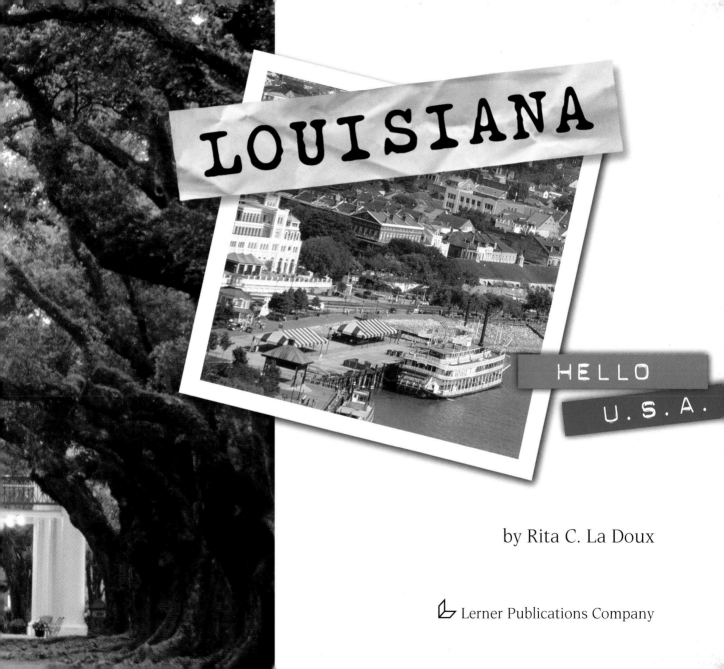

LOUISIANA

HELLO
U.S.A.

by Rita C. La Doux

Lerner Publications Company

You'll find this picture of American alligators at the beginning of each chapter in this book. Louisiana's state reptile is found in and near the state's lakes, swamps, and rivers. The creatures have sharp teeth, can grow to be 12 feet long, and often weigh up to 500 pounds. Some of them are even bigger—one alligator found in Vermilion Parish, Louisiana, during the 1890s was said to be more than 19 feet long.

Cover (left): A street in the French Quarter of New Orleans at night. Cover (right): Swamp cedars in the Atchafalaya Basin Bayou. Pages 2–3: Oak Alley Plantation in Vacherie, Louisiana. Page 3: View of the Mississippi River Delta and the French Quarter from the New Orleans Hilton.

This book is available in two editions:
Library binding by Lerner Publications Company, a division of Lerner Publishing Group
Soft cover by First Avenue Editions, an imprint of Lerner Publishing Group
241 First Avenue North
Minneapolis, MN 55401 U.S.A.

Website address: www.lernerbooks.com

Library of Congress Cataloging-in-Publication Data

LaDoux, Rita, 1951–
    Louisiana / by Rita C. La Doux. (Revised and expanded 2nd edition)
       p.   cm. — (Hello U.S.A.)
    Includes index.
    ISBN: 0–8225–4065–7 (lib. bdg. : alk. paper)
    ISBN: 0–8225–4145–9 (pbk. : alk. paper)
    1. Louisiana—Juvenile literature. [1. Louisiana.] I. Title. II. Series.
  F369.3 .L33 2002
    976.3—dc21   2001001738

Manufactured in the United States of America
1 2 3 4 5 6 – JR – 07 06 05 04 03 02

CONTENTS

Slow-moving streams known as bayous cover parts of Louisiana.

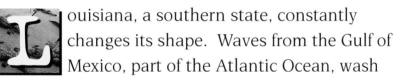

THE LAND

Plains, Bayous, and Delta

ouisiana, a southern state, constantly changes its shape. Waves from the Gulf of Mexico, part of the Atlantic Ocean, wash up onto the state's southern shore and carry small chunks of land back to the ocean. At the same time, the Mississippi River carries millions of tons of **sediment** (sand and soil) from the north into Louisiana.

As the Mississippi enters the Gulf, the river drops its load of sediment. The land formed by the buildup of sediment at the mouth of the Mississippi is called a delta. The Mississippi Delta makes up about one-fourth of the state.

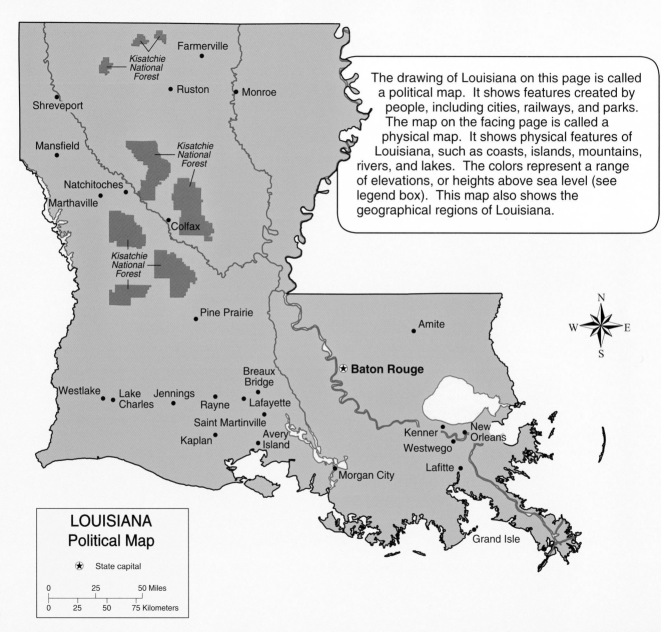

Farmerville

Kisatchie National Forest

Ruston

Monroe

Shreveport

Mansfield

Kisatchie National Forest

Natchitoches

Marthaville

Colfax

Kisatchie National Forest

Pine Prairie

The drawing of Louisiana on this page is called a political map. It shows features created by people, including cities, railways, and parks. The map on the facing page is called a physical map. It shows physical features of Louisiana, such as coasts, islands, mountains, rivers, and lakes. The colors represent a range of elevations, or heights above sea level (see legend box). This map also shows the geographical regions of Louisiana.

Amite

⭐ **Baton Rouge**

Breaux Bridge

Westlake Lake Charles Jennings Rayne Lafayette

Saint Martinville

Kaplan Avery Island

Kenner New Orleans

Westwego

Lafitte

Morgan City

Grand Isle

N
W E
S

LOUISIANA
Political Map

⭐ State capital

| 0 | 25 | 50 Miles |
| 0 | 25 | 50 | 75 Kilometers |

8

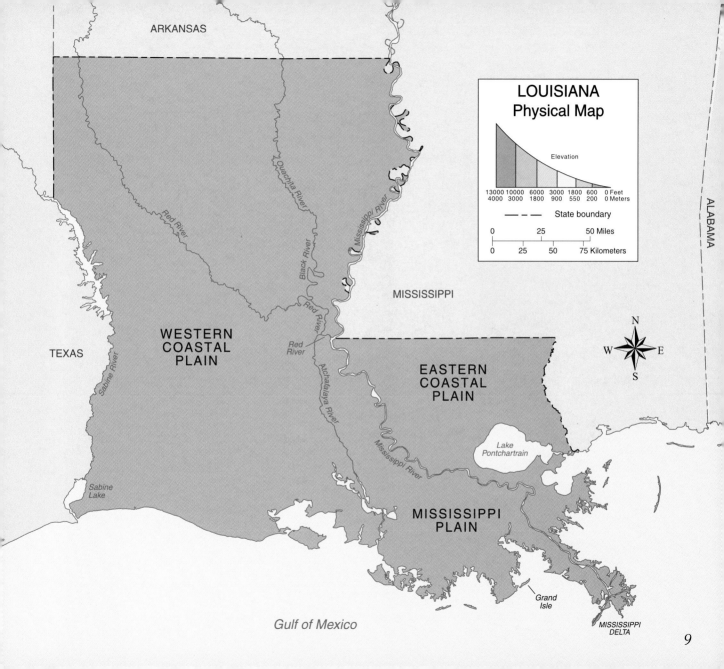

ARKANSAS

TEXAS

**WESTERN
COASTAL
PLAIN**

Red River

Ouachita River

Black River

Mississippi River

Red River

Red
River

Atchafalaya River

Sabine River

Sabine
Lake

Mississippi River

MISSISSIPPI

**EASTERN
COASTAL
PLAIN**

Lake
Pontchartrain

**MISSISSIPPI
PLAIN**

ALABAMA

Grand
Isle

*MISSISSIPPI
DELTA*

Gulf of Mexico

LOUISIANA
Physical Map

Elevation

| 13000 | 10000 | 6000 | 3000 | 1800 | 600 | 0 Feet |
| 4000 | 3000 | 1800 | 900 | 550 | 200 | 0 Meters |

– – – State boundary

0   25   50 Miles

0   25   50   75 Kilometers

N
W   E
S

Louisiana's rivers flow into the Gulf of Mexico.

Other rivers have also added land to Louisiana by dropping loads of sediment near the Gulf. In fact, long ago much of Louisiana was actually part of the Gulf of Mexico. But rivers carried enough sediment to fill part of the Gulf.

The Gulf of Mexico washes along Louisiana's entire southern border. The state shares its western border with Texas. The Mississippi River separates much of Louisiana from the state of Mississippi to the east. Arkansas sits to the north. Louisiana itself is divided into three land regions—the Western Coastal Plain, the Mississippi Plain, and the Eastern Coastal Plain.

The Western Coastal Plain is Louisiana's largest region, covering the entire western half of the state. In the northern part of this region, rivers flow between tree-covered hills. Driskill Mountain, the highest point in Louisiana, is located in the northern part of the state. To the south lies a wide band of grassland. South of the grassland are

wetlands, which include swamps (forested wetlands) and marshes (grassy wetlands). Between the wetlands and the Gulf of Mexico are beaches called barrier beaches. Deposits of oil and natural gas are found in the region's southern marshes and in the north around the city of Shreveport.

Louisiana has a lot of water, from rivers and lakes to marshes and swamps.

New Orleans, Louisiana, a city that lies on the Mississippi River, is a major port city in the southern United States.

The Mississippi Plain stretches along the Mississippi River from Louisiana's northern edge to the Gulf of Mexico. For centuries, the rich soils of this region were built up by sediment that the river dropped each time it flooded. New Orleans and Baton Rouge, the state's two largest cities, are located in the southern third of the Mississippi Plain. New Orleans is the lowest point in Louisiana at five feet below sea level.

In the southeastern corner of Louisiana lies the Eastern Coastal Plain. Marshes cover this region in the west and south, and prairies blanket the northeast. Once part of Florida, the Eastern Coastal Plain is often called the Florida Parishes. (In Louisiana, counties are called parishes.) Both saltwater and freshwater lakes dot

Louisiana. Lake Pontchartrain, north of New Orleans, is the state's largest lake. Louisiana also has many rivers and **bayous,** or slow-moving streams. Many of the bayous are in the Mississippi Delta. When the rivers in Louisiana flood, the bayous help drain away the overflow water. The state's most important rivers are the Mississippi, the Red, the Atchafalaya, the Ouachita, the Black, and the Sabine.

Warm, moist air travels north from the Gulf of Mexico and gives Louisiana hot and very humid weather. The average summer temperature is a steamy 82° F, but the thermometer has risen as high as 114° F. The mild winter temperatures average 55° F in the south and 49° F in the north.

Each year about 57 inches of rain fall on Louisiana, making it one of the wettest states in the country. In the late summer and early fall, hurricanes, or violent storms, form over the ocean. Some of the hurricanes blow in from the Gulf of Mexico and pound Louisiana's coast with heavy rains, high waves, and strong winds.

Louisiana's winters are mild, and snow doesn't stay on the ground for long.

Nutrias, with their webbed feet and long tails, swim in the swamps of Louisiana.

Louisiana's hot, wet weather makes the state a good home for many different types of plants and animals. About half of Louisiana is forested. The state's trees include hickory, magnolia, and pine. Spanish moss, a plant without roots, hangs from oak and bald cypress trees in southern Louisiana. Beautiful flowers such as honey-suckles, camellias, jasmines, and azaleas grow all over the state.

Deer, mink, raccoon, muskrats, opossums, and wild hogs live throughout Louisiana. Alligators and nutrias—small beaverlike animals—thrive in the southern swamps. Oysters and shrimp can be found in the state's coastal marshes. The marshes are also the year-round home of birds such as herons, bald eagles, and brown pelicans. Millions of ducks, geese, and other birds spend their winters in Louisiana.

Colorful hot air balloons float high above the Louisiana landscape.

Spanish moss hanging from the branches of giant oak trees is a common sight in Louisiana.

Some of Louisiana's birds, such as brown pelicans and bald eagles, used to be very few in numbers in the state. They were in danger of becoming extinct, or dying out. Due to the efforts of Louisianans, the numbers of these birds have gone up. Many bird species are protected in Louisiana's state parks and wildlife refuges, where they have a better chance to flourish.

THE HISTORY

The Bayou Blend

umbo—a spicy soup made of okra and a mix of other vegetables, ground sassafras leaves, and meat or seafood—is a specialty of Louisiana's cooks. Like gumbo, the history of the state is a spicy blend of stories and people.

The first people to live in North America were Indians, or Native Americans. Over time many different Indian groups made their way into the area that became Louisiana. By the 1600s, as many as 15,000 Indians were living in the area.

The Chitimacha built their villages on the Mississippi Delta. For food, they used blowguns to shoot alligators, turtles, and fish. The Caddo lived in what would become northwestern Louisiana. They hollowed out logs to make canoes and built tall houses from saplings and grass.

Servants carried the Natchez king—also known as the Great Sun—everywhere because his feet were not supposed to touch the ground. The Natchez were one of the earliest groups to live in Louisiana.

The Natchez, a group that lived near the Mississippi River, built their houses out of sun-baked mud and straw. The tribe's king, called the Great Sun, ruled over the Natchez from a village temple. The Natchez and their king didn't know it, but kings in European countries had sent explorers to claim land in North America.

In 1682 René-Robert Cavelier, Sieur de La Salle, a French explorer, reached the Gulf of Mexico. He claimed for France the Mississippi River and all the land around all the rivers that flow into it. He named the area Louisiana in honor of Louis XIV, the king of France. Louisiana stretched west from the Mississippi River to the Rocky Mountains, north into what later became Canada, and south to the Gulf.

The French sent soldiers, settlers, food, and supplies to the southern part of their new **colony,** or settlement. Few of the settlers were farmers, so France advertised for farmers in Germany, where many people grew crops for a living.

Germans soon began arriving in Louisiana. They built farms north of the French settlements and began to grow some of the colony's food. Some colonists used black slaves to work on their farms. The slaves were brought to the colony from Africa and from the West Indies, islands far to the south of Louisiana in the Caribbean Sea.

In 1682 the French explorer La Salle claimed a large territory for France and called it Louisiana.

The settlers got more food by trading guns, tools, and fabric with the Indians in the area. Unfortunately, the settlers also carried diseases that were deadly to the Indians. These diseases sometimes killed entire tribes.

Soon the settlers wanted to build homes and farms on the homeland of the Natchez Indians. In 1729 the colony's leaders ordered the tribe off of their land. The Natchez fought back in a war that became known as the Natchez Revolt. But the French overpowered the tribe. The few Indians who survived were sold into slavery or taken by other Indian tribes.

France was losing money on Louisiana. The French government had to buy goods, guns, and other supplies for the colonists. And Britain, which had a strong army and thousands of colonists in eastern North America, was threatening to take Louisiana away from France. So in 1762 France gave Louisiana to Spain, a country that was a friend to France, to keep it out of British control.

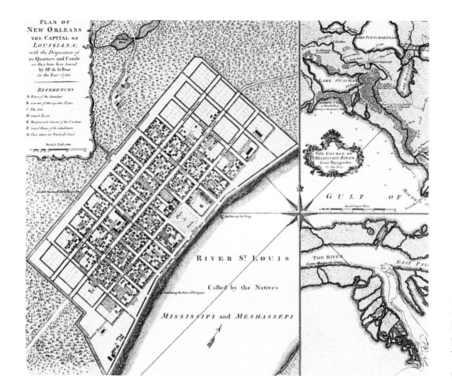

PLAN OF
NEW ORLEANS
THE CAPITAL OF
LOUISIANA;
with the Disposition of
its Quarters and Canals
as they have been traced
by Mr de la Tour
in the Year 1720.

REFERENCES
A. House of the Intendant
B. Convent of the Capuchin Fryars
C. The Ails
D. Guard Room
E. Hospital and Convent of the Ursulines
F. Guard House of the Inhabitants
G. Place where the Windmill Stood

French Fathoms

THE COURSE OF
THE MISSISSIPPI RIVER
from Bayagoulas
to the Sea

GULF OF

RIVER ST LOUIS

Called by the Natives

MISSISSIPI and MESHASSEPI

LAKE PONTCHARTRAIN

LAKE OUACHA

THE RIVER

EAST PAS

Before the 1760s,
maps of New Orleans
were printed in French.
This map was the first
one printed in English.

While under Spanish rule, Louisiana prospered.
Settlers living east of the Mississippi sent crops
down the river to the growing city of New Orleans,
where the crops were shipped to the eastern coast of
North America and to Europe. In exchange, manufactured goods were shipped from Europe to New
Orleans.

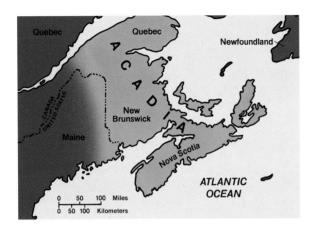

Many people moved from Acadia to Louisiana in the mid-1700s. Acadia later became part of eastern Canada.

Louisiana's population grew during Spain's rule. New settlers from France joined the **Creoles**—descendants of the earliest French and Spanish settlers, who lived in and around New Orleans. During the mid-1700s, the British forced French settlers out of their homes in Acadia, what later became part of eastern Canada. Many of these Acadians, called **Cajuns,** moved south to Louisiana, where they could speak French and practice their Catholic religion freely. And thousands of slaves continued to be shipped to Louisiana.

In 1800 Spain agreed to give Louisiana back to France. But just three years later, the French, who needed money, sold the huge territory to the United States in a deal called the Louisiana Purchase. The U.S. government then divided Louisiana into several smaller territories. On April 30, 1812, one of the territories—Louisiana—became the 18th state of the United States.

JEAN LAFITTE: Hero or Outlaw?

In 1813, during the War of 1812, Louisiana's governor offered a $500 reward for the capture of a pirate named Jean Lafitte. A Frenchman, Lafitte became well known in New Orleans, where he sold everything from slaves to silks and spices. To get his goods, Lafitte and his crew of ruthless smugglers attacked and took over European ships sailing in the Gulf of Mexico. People in New Orleans were eager to buy the stolen booty, and Lafitte became very rich.

By posting the reward, Louisiana's governor hoped to end Lafitte's raiding. But Great Britain had something else in mind. The British government wanted Jean Lafitte and his men to help capture New Orleans for Great Britain. The British offered Lafitte $30,000 and a pardon for his piracy if he would fight on their side. But Lafitte said no. Instead, he warned the U.S. government of the attack and helped U.S. general Andrew Jackson win the Battle of New Orleans on January 8, 1815. After the war, President James Madison pardoned Lafitte, whose efforts to save New Orleans had made him a war hero.

Many of Louisiana's immigrants came to the area to be able to have religious freedom. They built churches where they could practice their religions.

The white population in the new state included many groups besides Creoles and Cajuns. Some settlers had left more crowded states to the east. Others were **immigrants** from France, Germany, and the West Indies. Most of the black people were slaves, but some black Louisianans were free people of color, a group that included freed slaves and immigrants from the West Indies.

Although they came from many places, people in the new state fell into two main groups—those who had French backgrounds and those who didn't. The Cajuns and Creoles—who lived mainly in southern Louisiana—made up the largest group. They spoke French, had French ancestors, and practiced the Catholic religion. The second group lived mostly in the northern part of the state and in the Florida Parishes. Many of these Louisianans practiced Protestant religions, spoke English, and had British or German ancestors.

In the early 1800s, the first steamboat in North America arrived at the port of New Orleans.

Steamboats carrying bales of cotton to market were a common sight in the 1800s.

Steamboats traveled faster and carried more cargo than the old riverboats. Soon more goods were flowing though the city than ever before.

Dock workers unloaded ships that arrived from Europe and the East Coast. Merchants and traders bought the goods and sent them on steamboats up the Mississippi River to be resold. The boats returned to New Orleans filled with grain, cotton, and tobacco. Workers loaded the crops onto ships headed to northern states and to Europe.

New Orleans provided housing and entertainment for the large number of travelers, sailors, and merchants who passed through. The city offered everything from opera and theater to dancing and gambling, or betting on games.

The people of New Orleans attended opera houses for entertainment.

Most people in Louisiana lived in the country and worked on farms. Sugarcane was grown in southern Louisiana on plantations, or large farms worked by slaves. Plantations farther north grew cotton. Many farmers in southern Louisiana owned plantations, but most of the state's northern farms were small.

Louisiana's planters were not the only ones to use slaves. Plantations all over the South depended on slave labor. But by the 1850s, many people in the United States were opposing slavery. Slavery was illegal in Northern states, and many Northern politicians were trying to end slavery in the South.

Louisiana's plantation owners lived in large, elegantly furnished homes, while most slaves lived in small, crowded quarters with dirt floors and no furniture.

Free People of Color

In 1820 almost half of New Orleans's 29,000 residents were black people. As in the rest of Louisiana, many people in New Orleans believed white people were superior to black people. New Orleans's society was divided into groups. At the top were white people and at the bottom were slaves. In between were free black people, also called free people of color.

Some slaves were able to gain their freedom. Slave owners sometimes released slaves who had been hardworking and loyal. Or, if a slave owner had children with one of his slaves, he would usually free the woman and the children. Other slaves were able to buy their freedom, either with money earned doing extra work or with help from freed relatives. Most free people of color in Louisiana lived in New Orleans, where the women could find work as nurses, hairdressers, dressmakers, laundresses, and street vendors. Free black men had jobs as shoemakers, bartenders, laborers, and businessmen.

Free people of color had some rights. They could take an oath in court, make a will, and own property. But they were not allowed to vote, hold public office, or practice law. And whenever they signed official documents—such as wills—they had to add "colored man" or "colored woman" after their signature. Not until 1865, when the 13th Amendment to the U.S. Constitution made slavery illegal, were all African Americans free people of color.

Freed slave children pose in their finest school clothes in about 1863.

By January 1861, several Southern states, including Louisiana, had withdrawn from the United States and had formed the Confederate States of America, a separate country that allowed slavery. President Abraham Lincoln wanted to keep the country together. But disagreements continued, and soon the Civil War had begun.

Union, or Northern, troops took over New Orleans in 1862. One year later, they overpowered Confederate forts along the Mississippi River. Union control of the river made it very difficult for Confederates to send food and weapons to their troops.

By 1865, when the Confederacy admitted defeat, homes, barns, roads, and railroads had been destroyed in Louisiana. Many residents had no food, work, or shelter. Slaves had been freed, but most of them had no way to make a living.

To make matters worse, many Northern merchants started using railroads instead of steamboats to ship their goods. The port of New Orleans lost much of its prewar business.

After the Civil War, African American men won the right to vote. Here, men register to vote in Caddo Parish.

In 1867 U.S. troops from the North moved into Louisiana to oversee **Reconstruction,** or the rebuilding of the South. These troops forced white Louisianans to follow a new U.S. law that gave all black men the right to vote.

When the U.S. soldiers left in 1877, some Louisianans were afraid that the right to vote would give black people too much power. These white Louisianans threatened or attacked blacks who tried to vote. By 1900 Louisiana had passed laws that took the vote away from African American men and from poor white men. The state also passed laws that separated black people from white people in schools, on trains, in restaurants, and at public events such as circuses.

By 1900 most Louisianans were still working on farms, but new industries had begun to develop. One was logging. The state's thick forests drew logging companies from northern states, where most of the forests had already been cut. The logging companies built sawmills and hired thousands of Louisianans to chop down the state's trees and cut them into boards.

Louisiana's first oil well was drilled near Jennings in 1901. Soon workers were drilling wells all over the western half of the state. Oil refineries, or factories where oil is cleaned and made into gasoline and other products, were built around Baton Rouge and Shreveport. The refineries employed many more Louisianans.

Oil was first discovered in Louisiana in the town of Jennings, where these oil wells are located.

The logging industry employed many Louisianans. Workers chopped down trees and trains hauled the logs to sawmills.

In the early 1900s, most people in Louisiana lived in areas that could be reached only by dirt roads, which were often muddy and impossible to travel. Many rural, white Louisianans could not get an education because very few schools existed. Even fewer schools were open for black students.

In 1928 a Louisianan named Huey Long ran for governor. Long promised to tax oil and logging companies and to spend the money to help the state's poor people. Long won the election.

To turn his promises into laws, Long filled the state government with people who were loyal to him. He soon controlled Louisiana's government completely. He was very popular with people he helped, but he was hated by those who thought he had too much power. Long became a U.S. senator in 1930. He planned to run for president of the United States, but he was assassinated in 1935.

Louisiana's most famous governor, Huey Long *(right),* worked to help poor people and was known for saying "Every Man a King."

Books for Everyone

Both black and white Louisianans benefited from changes Huey Long made when he was governor. Long built roads, bridges, and hospitals. He expanded library services, provided free text books for schoolchildren, and started a program to help adults learn to read and write.

Huey Long's accomplishments while governor of Louisiana included expanding library services to include bookmobiles. Here, a group of Louisianans pose in front of the Webster Parish Library on wheels.

Louisiana's factories began building ships for the U.S. Navy during World War II.

The outbreak of World War II (1939–1945) brought more jobs and money into the state. Louisiana's oil was needed to fuel tanks and airplanes. And New Orleans bustled as workers loaded ships with supplies needed by the soldiers fighting in Europe.

During the war, the lives of Louisianans improved. During the **civil rights movement** of the 1960s, black citizens were once again guaranteed the right to vote in Louisiana. African American students also won the right to attend the same schools as white students. Over the years, many black politicians were elected to government offices, and in 1978 Ernest ("Dutch") Morial became the first black mayor of New Orleans.

Louisiana's oil industry boomed during the 1970s, bringing a lot of money into the state. But by the 1980s, the industry was making less money. State leaders have been trying to attract other businesses to Louisiana so that the state doesn't have to rely only on the success of the oil industry.

Louisiana is also working to protect the state's natural environment. Each year the state loses miles of coastal wetlands. To help stop this loss,

Tanks store oil for future use. Louisiana makes more money from oil than any state except for Texas.

Louisiana's wetlands are a precious resource for the state.

the U.S. Congress passed the Coastal Wetlands Planning, Protection, and Restoration Act in 1990. This fund provides federal grants to restore wetlands. Although problems remain, Louisianans are working together to try to solve them.

Louisiana has had to deal with corruption in the governor's office. In 1992 Edwin W. Edwards was elected to a fourth term as governor of Louisiana. But in 2000 it was discovered that Edwards had been breaking the law by conducting illegal business practices while he was governor. In response to this problem, Louisianans are working to promote honesty in their government.

PEOPLE & ECONOMY

Festivals, Food, and Fun

The French, Spanish, and African peoples of Louisiana have given the state a flavor all its own. European-style buildings and regional foods and music reflect the state's unique character.

Northern and southern Louisianans still have their differences, but the state is no longer split between English and French speakers. About 63 percent of Louisianans are white. Black Louisianans make up about 32 percent of the population. Smaller groups of people in the state include Latinos, Native Americans, and Asian Americans.

About 1 percent of Louisiana's population are Native Americans.

The architecture of New Orleans reflects its French history.

Almost 4.5 million people live in Louisiana, mostly in urban areas. The largest city in Louisiana is New Orleans. Baton Rouge, the next largest, is the state capital. Shreveport and Monroe are in the north. Lafayette and Lake Charles, in the south, are not far from the Gulf coast.

Every year the cities and towns of Louisiana come alive with festivals. Ruston celebrates peaches in June, Farmerville honors watermelons in July, and Colfax pays respect to pecans in November.

But the state's most famous festival is Mardi Gras, held in New Orleans and other towns in southern Louisiana. Mardi Gras is a festival held on the day before the beginning of Lent, a period of fasting before Easter. In the weeks leading up to Mardi Gras, musicians and wildly dressed people parade down the streets on floats and dance at costume balls.

Festivals also celebrate the music of Louisiana. Marthaville hosts the Louisiana State Fiddling Contest each April. New Orleans, the birthplace of jazz, holds the Jazz and Heritage Festival each spring. Jazz artists perform nightly at Preservation Hall in New Orleans.

Mardi Gras parades include inventive floats, such as this giant alligator, that reflect the state's history, wildlife, and economy.

In Shreveport, a father and daughter peel crayfish at a festival that honors the lobsterlike shellfish.

At Lafayette's Festivals Acadiens, held each September, musicians play Cajun tunes. Another type of music native to Louisiana is zydeco, which combines rock and roll with Cajun and African American sounds.

Along with Louisiana's unique music comes its spicy and unusual food. Restaurants feature local shrimp, crab, oysters, crayfish, and fish in dishes such as jambalaya (spicy rice with seafood or meat) and gumbo.

Cajun musicians of all ages perform at a pig roast in Ossun, Louisiana (*left*). The Preservation Hall Jazz Band performs in the French Quarter of New Orleans (*below*).

A young boater crosses a small lake in a pirogue, or canoe.

Football fans go wild in the Superdome, home of the New Orleans Saints—Louisiana's only professional sports team. Every New Year's Day, two of the best college football teams in the nation clash in the Sugar Bowl game at the Superdome.

Louisianans also like to play sports. Rodeos, horse races, and pirogue (canoe) races draw participants and fans from around the state and the nation. Many people enjoy fishing in the state's bayous, in its lakes, and in the Gulf of Mexico. Bayou cruises and swamp tours, which are offered throughout the state, give visitors a chance to see unusual birds, alligators, and other wetland wildlife.

Louisianans work at many different kinds of jobs. Most—61 percent—work at service jobs. People with service jobs help other people or businesses. Service workers include cashiers, bankers, and waitpeople. Government workers make up 17 percent of working Louisianans. Government workers include people like park rangers and post-office workers.

Shipping is an important source of service jobs in Louisiana. Barges loaded with grain, oil, and chemicals travel down the state's rivers to the port of New Orleans. Ship pilots bring cargo into New Orleans from around the world. Workers called stevedores load and unload the barges and ships, and traders buy and sell the goods. Truck drivers deliver some of the goods to local stores, and salespeople sell the items to customers.

The historic French Quarter of New Orleans boasts a variety of delicious foods.

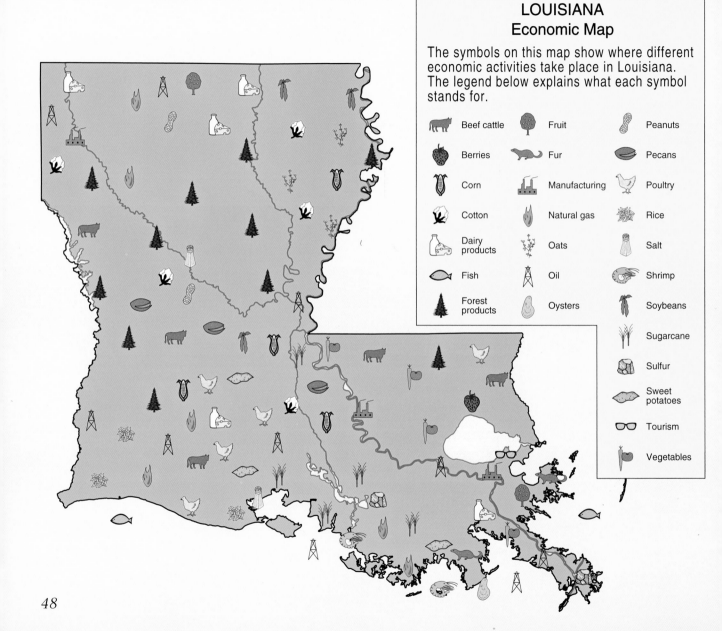

LOUISIANA
Economic Map

The symbols on this map show where different economic activities take place in Louisiana. The legend below explains what each symbol stands for.

Beef cattle	Fruit	Peanuts
Berries	Fur	Pecans
Corn	Manufacturing	Poultry
Cotton	Natural gas	Rice
Dairy products	Oats	Salt
Fish	Oil	Shrimp
Forest products	Oysters	Soybeans
		Sugarcane
		Sulfur
		Sweet potatoes
		Tourism
		Vegetables

Only 3 percent of Louisiana's workers earn money from agriculture, but farmers plant crops on about one-third of the state's land. In southern Louisiana, farmers grow rice in flooded fields. In the valleys of the Red and Mississippi Rivers, farmers raise soybeans, cotton, and sugarcane. In northern Louisiana, pine and oak trees are planted for future logging. And in ponds throughout the state, farmers raise crayfish and catfish to sell to restaurants and grocery stores.

A barge heads down the Mississippi River to the river delta in Louisiana.

Workers drill for oil *(left)* in the Gulf of Mexico. The oil is sent to refineries *(above)* in cities such as Baton Rouge and Westlake.

Louisiana's most important seafoods—shrimp and oysters—come from the Gulf of Mexico. Louisiana's fishers bring in nearly one-fourth of all the seafood caught in the United States.

The Gulf of Mexico is also rich in oil. Each year, workers pump millions of barrels of oil and natural gas in the Gulf and throughout the state. Louisiana supplies about one-fourth of the oil and one-third of the natural gas mined in the United States. Only 3 percent of working Louisianans have mining jobs, but these people earn about 18 percent of the state's money.

Nine percent of Louisiana's workers have jobs in manufacturing. They process products from the state's farming, logging, fishing, and mining industries into finished goods. People at food processing plants pack seafood. Mill workers cut trees into lumber or grind wood into pulp for paper. Workers at refineries mix oil products with other chemicals to make fertilizers and plastics. And Louisiana's shipbuilders make boats that transport these products to markets all over the world.

THE ENVIRONMENT

Protecting the Wetlands

 ouisiana's wetlands are among the state's most valuable natural resources. More than 1 million Louisianans earn their living from wetlands, and almost 1.5 million of the state's residents make their homes in wetland areas. But Louisiana is losing many of its coastal wetlands to erosion, a process in which water washes away loose soil.

The marshes that are eroding have been very important to the state's economy. People catch fish and shellfish that lay eggs in the coastal marshes. Louisiana's seafood brings almost $315 million into the state every year.

Louisiana's coastal wetlands *(opposite page)* are home to many creatures, such as alligators *(right)*.

Many northern birds, such as Canada geese *(facing page)*, spend the winter in Louisiana's marshes *(right)*.

In the state's swamps, trappers catch nutrias and sell their fur. Hunters, fishers, and tourists in wetland areas spend millions of dollars at Louisiana's restaurants, motels, and stores each year.

Coastal marshes are very important to wildlife and plants, too. Millions of ducks and geese depend on Louisiana's marshes for food and shelter in the winter. Other birds rest and feed in the marshes while traveling to their winter or summer homes. Some types of plants in Louisiana's marshes cannot grow anywhere else in the United States.

Coastal marshes also protect inland towns from the full force of hurricanes. As hurricane winds pass over the marshes, the storms slow down, causing less damage when they finally hit inland towns. Marshes also hold some of the water that would otherwise flood coastal towns when storms strike.

The ocean waves that lap against Louisiana's coast have eroded marshes naturally for thousands of years. But the Mississippi River also dropped tons of soil all along its banks each time it flooded. The sediment was then carried by smaller rivers and streams into the marshes, where the soil settled, repairing the damage caused by the ocean.

In the late 1800s, the marshes started eroding faster than they could be rebuilt. As people built homes and farms along the Mississippi, they also built **levees,** or walls that keep rivers from flooding. When the river stopped flooding, no sediment replaced marshland that had washed away.

The levees also made the river straighter, which causes it to flow faster. Since the levees were built, the Mississippi River has flowed so fast into the Gulf of Mexico that much of its sediment gets carried out to deep Gulf waters instead of settling in marshes.

Mining practices also cause coastal marshes to erode. Much of Louisiana's oil and natural gas is found in coastal marshes. To get to these fuels, workers dig canals through marshes.

When storms blow water toward the coast, the long, straight canals let the seawater travel far into the marshes. The salty Gulf water kills plants that can only grow in the fresh water of the marshes. Without plant roots to hold soil in place, waves wash the soil away. The water then becomes too deep for marsh plants and animals, and the marsh becomes an open pond or lake.

Louisiana is losing at least 25 to 35 square miles of coastal marshes every year. At this rate, by 2009, wetlands the size of San Diego will be lost. To try to save this area, Louisianans started the Wetlands

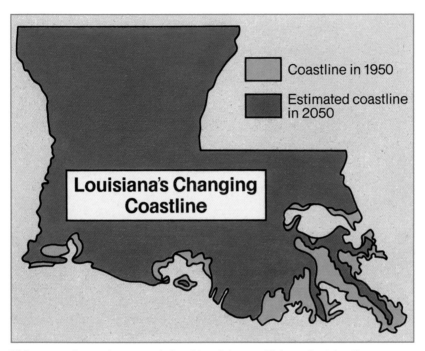

Louisiana's Changing Coastline

Coastline in 1950

Estimated coastline in 2050

This map shows how much land Louisiana will have lost by the year 2050 if the state continues to lose coastal marshes as fast as it has since 1950.

Conservation and Restoration Fund in 1989. This fund gives millions of dollars each year to projects that will protect Louisiana's wetlands.

In one of the programs paid for by the fund, workers have cut into levees along the Mississippi River to let water and soil flood the wetlands.

In another program, two rows of fences are built close together along the coast. Dead Christmas trees are then stacked between the fences. When water moves through the fences, the trees break the waves and hold the soil. The deposits of soil become islands. Plants begin to grow on the islands, and eventually the islands become a new marsh.

Workers stack Christmas trees between fences. The blockade traps soil needed for plants to grow and helps create new marshes.

To help prevent marsh soil from eroding, workers plant grasses.

When mining companies are finished using a canal, they must plug it at both ends or fill it so that salt water cannot get into the canal. Sometimes workers plant marsh grasses on the former canal. The roots of the plants slow erosion by holding soil in place.

All of these efforts have saved or rebuilt marshes, but erosion continues. As Louisianans keep finding ways to restore marshes, they give coastal marshes a better chance to survive.

ALL ABOUT LOUISIANA

White alligator

Fun Facts

The 150,000 alligators in Louisiana have a few special cousins. The state is home to the only known white alligators in the world.

The longest boxing match ever took place in New Orleans on April 6–7, 1893. Andy Bowen and Jack Burke boxed for 110 rounds, sparring for 7 hours and 19 minutes. The fight ended in a draw.

Tabasco pepper sauce was invented and is still made on Avery Island, Louisiana. The company was started in 1868, when Edmund McIlhenny first grew red peppers near his home on the island and bottled the hot, spicy sauce.

French traditions have a strong influence on Louisiana's state government. Unlike other states, Louisiana bases its laws on a code written by the French emperor Napoleon Bonaparte in 1804.

The world's largest private fleet of helicopters takes off once a week from Morgan City, Louisiana. The helicopters carry workers to and from shifts at offshore oil wells.

More crayfish are harvested in Louisiana than any other place in the world. About 87 percent of the United States's crayfish come from hatcheries in this state.

STATE SONG

Louisiana adopted two official state songs in 1977. "Give Me Louisiana" celebrates the state's natural features and its heritage. "You Are My Sunshine" is a country-and-western standard. Both songs were adopted by the state legislature in 1977.

GIVE ME LOUISIANA

Words and music by Doralice Fontane

Give me Loui - si - an - a, The state where I was born The state of snow - y cot - ton, The best I've ev - er known; A state of sweet mag - no - lias, And cre - ole mel - o - dies Oh give me Loui - si - an - a, The state where I was born Oh what sweet old mem - 'ries The mos - sy old oaks bring. It brings us the sto - ry of our E - van - ge - line A state of old tra - di - tion, of old plan - ta - tion days Makes good old Loui - si - an - a The sweet - est of all states.

You can hear "Give Me Louisiana" by visiting this website:
<http://www.50states.com/songs/louis/htm>

A LOUISIANA RECIPE

Gumbo, a spicy soup, is a traditional Louisiana dish. Gumbo reflects the state's Creole heritage—the word *gumbo* comes from an African word for okra.

GUMBO

Ask an adult for help with chopping and frying the ingredients.

3 tablespoons vegetable oil
3 tablespoons flour
1 large chopped onion
1 cup chopped celery
5–6 cloves
1 cup chopped green pepper
1 can tomato sauce
1 pound okra, sliced (frozen or fresh)

1 can tomatoes
2–3 cups water
1 teaspoon of sugar
salt and pepper to taste
2 pounds deveined, shelled shrimp
1 bay leaf
1 tablespoon chopped parsley

1. In heavy cast-iron skillet, heat vegetable oil. Slowly stir in flour. Continue stirring until flour is browned. Add onion, celery, cloves, and green pepper. Stir until heated through.
2. Add tomato sauce. Stir until mixture is crumbly and somewhat dry.
3. In another skillet, fry okra until no longer sticky or stringy. (You can also do this ahead of time.)
4. Add tomatoes and fried okra to large mixture. Cook slowly, adding 2–3 cups of water a little bit at a time. Add sugar and sprinkling of salt and pepper for seasoning.
5. Let the dish cook over low heat for about an hour. Add shrimp and bay leaf and cook for an additional 30 minutes. Serve over boiled or steamed rice and garnish with parsley.

HISTORICAL TIMELINE

10,000 B.C. Native Americans enter what later became Louisiana.

A.D. 1682 La Salle claims Louisiana for France.

1729 Natchez Indians revolt against the French.

1762 France gives the area of Louisiana to Spain.

1800 Spain gives Louisiana back to France.

1803 France sells territory that includes Louisiana to the United States in a deal called the Louisiana Purchase.

1812 Louisiana becomes the 18th state.

1815 The United States wins the Battle of New Orleans during the War of 1812 (1812–1815).

1861 The Civil War begins; Louisiana joins the Confederate States of America.

1862 Union troops take over New Orleans.

1865 The Union wins the Civil War; the 13th Amendment makes slavery illegal and frees Louisiana's slaves.

1900 Louisiana's logging industry develops, creating many new jobs.

1901 Workers drill Louisiana's first oil well in Jennings.

1928 Huey Long is elected governor.

1935 Huey Long is assassinated.

1960 Black students and white students begin attending the same elementary schools.

1970 The oil industry booms.

1977 Voters in New Orleans elect the city's first African American mayor.

1989 Louisianans create the Wetlands Conservation and Restoration Fund.

1992 Hurricane Andrew strikes Louisiana, causing the deaths of 11 people and about $1 billion in damages to property.

2000 Edwin W. Edwards is found guilty of conducting illegal business practices while governor.

OUTSTANDING LOUISIANANS

Louis Armstrong

Terry Bradshaw

Truman Capote

Harry Connick Jr.

Louis Armstrong (1900–1971) was a jazz musician and bandleader. Born in New Orleans, Armstrong was a world-class trumpet player. He became so popular that postal carriers delivered letters addressed only to Louis Armstrong, Mr. Jazz, U.S.A.

Terry Bradshaw (born 1948), from Shreveport, Louisiana, played football for the Pittsburgh Steelers from 1970 to 1984. The popular quarterback led the team to win four Super Bowls. Bradshaw works as a sports commentator on *FOX NFL Sunday*.

Truman Capote (1924–1984) was an author who was born in New Orleans. A great storyteller during his lifetime, Capote is known for novels such as *In Cold Blood* and *Breakfast at Tiffany's*, both of which were made into movies in the 1960s.

Harry Connick Jr. (born 1967) started playing the piano at the age of three. Born in New Orleans, Connick became a world-famous pianist and singer with his own 30-piece orchestra. He has won two Grammy Awards and has also acted in movies, including *Little Man Tate* and *Hope Floats*.

Jose Ruiz De Rivera (1904–1985), a sculptor from West Baton Rouge, Louisiana, created artworks by heating and molding thick steel rods. He formed rounded pieces, buffed them to a shine, and placed them on turning bases. De Rivera's work is displayed in some of the country's best-known museums.

Fats Domino (born 1928), from New Orleans, sings music that is a blend of the blues and rock and roll. In 1956 he recorded the hit song "Blueberry Hill."

Fats Domino

Ron Guidry (born 1950) pitched for the New York Yankees baseball team. In 1978 he won 25 games, winning the Cy Young Award for best pitcher in the American League. Guidry, born in Lafayette, Louisiana, is called Louisiana Lightning for his fast pitches.

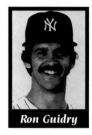

Ron Guidry

Lillian Hellman (1905–1984) was a playwright from New Orleans. Her works include *The Children's Hour* (1934), *Little Foxes* (1939), *Toys in the Attic* (1960), and the memoir *An Unfinished Woman* (1969).

Jerome Hunsaker (1886–1984), from Creston, Louisiana, designed and built aircraft. In 1914 he built the first working wind tunnel, which tests the effects of wind pressure on airplanes in flight.

Clementine Hunter (1887–1988) was an artist who grew up on a plantation near New Orleans. Hunter's simple and colorful oil paintings—done on cardboard, plywood, and brown paper bags—show the daily lives of black plantation workers.

Clementine Hunter

Mahalia Jackson (1911–1972), from New Orleans, is considered one of the best gospel singers ever. She got her start singing in church choirs. Jackson's 1947 recording of "Move On Up a Little Higher" made her a gospel star. She achieved more fame by singing "Amazing Grace" and other inspirational songs at many rallies held by Dr. Martin Luther King Jr. during the civil rights movement.

Mahalia Jackson

William Joyce

William Joyce (born 1957), from Shreveport, Louisiana, writes and illustrates children's stories. His books include *Dinosaur Bob and His Adventures with the Family Lazardo*, *A Day with Wilbur Robinson*, and *George Shrinks*.

Jean Lafitte (1780?–1825?) was a French pirate based in New Orleans. During the War of 1812, British officers asked him to help attack New Orleans. Instead Lafitte aided the U.S. side. After the war, Lafitte went back to robbing ships until he disappeared around 1825.

Dorothy Lamour

Dorothy Lamour (1914–1996), from New Orleans, Louisiana, was a famous actress both in Hollywood and on Broadway. Her credits include the films *The Jungle Princess* (1936), *Road to Singapore* (1940), *The Greatest Show on Earth* (1952), and plays *Roger the Sixth* (1951), *Oh! Captain* (1958), and *Hello, Dolly!* (1967).

Earl Long

Earl Long (1895–1960) and **Huey Long** (1893–1935) were born near Winnfield, Louisiana. Huey served as the state's governor from 1928 to 1932. For the next three years, he served as one of Louisiana's U.S. senators. Huey's brother Earl was the state's governor three different times in the 1940s and 1950s. The Long family was very powerful in Louisiana's politics, making friends as well as fierce enemies.

Huey Long

Wynton Marsalis (born 1961) is a trumpet player from New Orleans who plays both classical and jazz music. In 1984 he became the first musician to win Grammy Awards for his recordings of both types of music.

Jelly Roll Morton (1885–1941) was born in Gulfport, Louisiana. Morton played the piano and wrote and arranged music for jazz bands. Morton is known for many compositions, including "Jelly Roll Blues" and "King Porter Stomp."

Mel Ott

Mel Ott (1909–1958) played baseball with the New York Giants from 1926 to 1947. Ott, who was born in Gretna, Louisiana, hit 511 home runs during his career. He was elected to the National Baseball Hall of Fame in 1951.

Edward Perkins (born 1928) became the first black U.S. ambassador to the country of South Africa in 1986. After his term, Perkins was appointed director general of the Foreign Service and director of personnel for the Department of State. Perkins was born in Sterlington, Louisiana.

Edward Perkins

Cokie Roberts (born 1943), from New Orleans, Louisiana, became chief congressional analyst for ABC News in 1998. In addition to providing political commentary for such shows as *World News Tonight*, Roberts co-hosts the ABC news broadcast *This Week with Sam Donaldson & Cokie Roberts*, and is a news analyst for National Public Radio.

Bill Russell

Bill Russell (born 1934), a basketball player and coach, is from Monroe, Louisiana. Known for his defense skills, Russell played center for the Boston Celtics from 1956 to 1969. He became the first black coach in the National Basketball Association and was elected to the National Basketball Hall of Fame in 1975.

Hank Williams Jr. (born 1949), from Shreveport, Louisiana, has been a well-known country-western singer since the 1960s. In 1987 and 1988 he was named the Country Music Entertainer of the Year.

Hank Williams Jr.

FACTS-AT-A-GLANCE

Nickname: Pelican State

Songs: "Give Me Louisiana" and "You Are My Sunshine"

Motto: Union, Justice, and Confidence

Flower: magnolia

Tree: bald cypress

Bird: brown pelican

Dog: Catahoula Leopard Dog

Insect: honeybee

Fossil: petrified palmwood

Gemstone: agate

Date and ranking of statehood: April 30, 1812, the 18th state

Capital: Baton Rouge

Area: 43,566 square miles

Rank in area, nationwide: 33rd

Average January temperature: 50° F

Average July temperature: 82° F

On Louisiana's state flag, a pelican feeds her young. Many brown pelicans live along the state's coast, and Louisiana is sometimes called the Pelican State.

POPULATION GROWTH

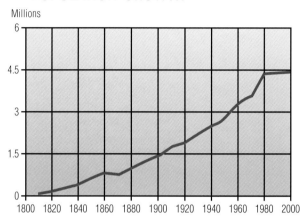

Millions

This chart shows how Louisiana's population has grown from 1810 until 2000.

Louisiana's state seal shows a pelican—the state bird—tending to three young chicks. "Union, Justice, and Confidence," the motto of Louisiana, surrounds the birds.

Population: 4,468,976 (2000 census)

Rank in population, nationwide: 22nd

Major cities and populations: (2000 census) New Orleans (484,674), Baton Rouge (227,818), Shreveport (200,145), Lafayette (110,257), Lake Charles (71,757)

U.S. senators: 2

U.S. representatives: 7

Electoral votes: 9

Natural resources: lumber, natural gas, oil, salt, soil, sulfur

Agricultural products: beef cattle, corn, cotton, dairy cattle, rice, soybeans, strawberries, sugarcane, sweet potatoes

Fishing industry: catfish, crayfish, menhaden, oysters, shrimp

Manufactured goods: fertilizers, food products, paint, paper products, plastics, ships

WHERE LOUISIANANS WORK

Services—61 percent (services includes jobs in trade; community, social and personal services; finance, insurance, and real estate; transportation, communication, and utilities)

Government—17 percent

Manufacturing—9 percent

Construction—7 percent

Mining—3 percent

Agriculture and fishing—3 percent

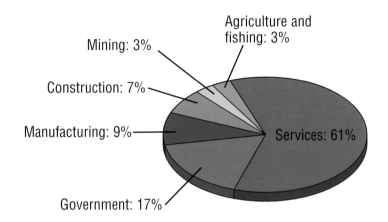

Mining: 3%

Agriculture and fishing: 3%

Construction: 7%

Manufacturing: 9%

Services: 61%

Government: 17%

GROSS STATE PRODUCT

Services—48 percent

Manufacturing—18 percent

Mining—18 percent

Government—11 percent

Construction—4 percent

Agriculture and fishing—1 percent

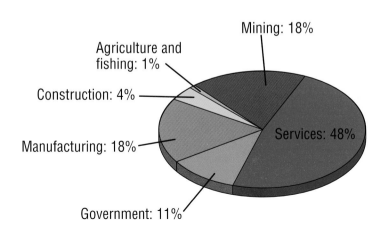

Mining: 18%

Agriculture and fishing: 1%

Construction: 4%

Manufacturing: 18%

Services: 48%

Government: 11%

STATE WILDLIFE

Mammals: beaver, deer, gray fox, mink, muskrat, nutria, opossum, rabbit, raccoon, skunk, wildcats, wild hog

Birds: bald eagle, brown pelican, doves, ducks, egrets, geese, herons, quails, wild turkey

Amphibians and reptiles: alligators, lizards, snakes, turtles

Fish: bass, blue crab, catfish, gaspergou, giant ray, oysters, shrimp, sunfish

Trees: cypress, hickory, longleaf pine, magnolia, oak, shortleaf pine

Wild plants: azaleas, camellias, honeysuckle, jasmine, lilies, orchids, Spanish moss

Cypress trees are found throughout Louisiana.

PLACES TO VISIT

Acadian Village, Lafayette
> This village consists of authentic Acadian houses. A restaurant and an art gallery showing only Acadian art are close by.

Aquarium of the Americas, New Orleans
> This aquarium hosts the largest collection of sharks and jellyfish in the United States. It also features a 400,000-gallon exhibit housing sea-life from the Gulf of Mexico.

Avery Island, near Iberia
> This island is the top of a huge underground salt dome. Tabasco, a hot pepper sauce, is made on the island.

Cypress Swamp Tours, Westwego
> Experience the wetlands and wildlife of Louisiana on a boat tour of Bayou Segnette. A local guide leads this tour, which includes viewing plantation houses, cemeteries, and alligators.

Feliciana Country
> This area includes the parishes of the East and West Feliciana. John J. Audubon, the famous naturalist and painter, made many sketches of this region. The area is also home to many old plantation homes.

French Quarter, New Orleans
> The oldest section of New Orleans, the French Quarter has attractions that include restaurants, French-style architecture, and museums.

Grand Isle, near New Orleans

Descendants of the pirate crew of Jean Lafitte live in the village on this island, which is located at the entrance to Barataria Bay.

Lake Fausse Pointe State Park, near Saint Martinville

Located on the edge of the Atchafalaya Basin, this park has cabins, campgrounds, trails, and playgrounds. Visitors can explore the park by canoe, but they must be careful not to get lost in the bayous.

Louisiana Purchase Gardens and Zoo, Monroe

The zoo is home to almost 500 exotic animals. Nature lovers can take a train ride though the exhibits and explore the beautifully landscaped gardens.

Oaklawn Manor, near Franklin

The house, the largest and grandest example of Greek Revival architecture in the area, is home to the state's governor.

Original Swamp Gardens, Morgan City

A guided walking tour through 3.5 acres of natural swamp offers a glimpse of life in the great Atchafalaya Swamp and a chance to see native animals such as nutrias, otters, and alligators.

Greenwood Plantation in Feliciana Country

ANNUAL EVENTS

Mardi Gras, New Orleans and other cities—*February and March*

Bonne Fête, Baton Rouge—*March*

Oyster Festival, Amite—*March*

Boggy Bayou Festival, Pine Prairie—*April*

Holiday in Dixie, Shreveport—*April*

Crawfish Festival, Breaux Bridge—*May*

Jazz and Gumbo Festival, Shreveport—*May*

Louisiana Blueberry Festival, Mansfield—*June*

World Champion Pirogue Races, Lafitte—*June*

Bastille Day, Kaplan—*July*

Frog Festival, Rayne—*September*

Louisiana State Fair, Shreveport—*October and November*

LEARN MORE ABOUT LOUISIANA

BOOKS

General

Frandin, Dennis Brindell, and Judith Bloom Brindell. *Louisiana.* Chicago: Children's Press, 1996.

Hintz, Martin. *Louisiana.* Danbury, CT: Children's Press, 1998. For older readers.

Thompson, Kathleen. *Louisiana.* Austin, TX: Raintree/Steck-Vaughn, 1996.

Special Interest

Grimm, Phyllis W. *Crayfish*. Minneapolis, MN: Lerner Publications Company, 2001. This easy reader details the life cycle of this plentiful crustacean.

Hoyt-Goldsmith, Diane. *Mardi Gras: A Cajun Country Celebration.* New York: Holiday House, 1995. A photo essay and introduction to a Cajun Mardi Gras celebration, including history, music, and food.

Hunter, Clementine, and Mary E. Lyons. *Talking with Tebe: Clementine Hunter, Memory Artist.* New York: Houghton-Mifflin Co., 1998. Clementine Hunter was an extraordinary artist who lived on a Louisiana plantation doing strenuous labor in Louisiana at the turn of the century. This book is a collection of her art and interviews.

Reneaux, J.J. *Cajun Folktales.* Des Moines, IA: August House Publishing, 1992. The author retells traditional Cajun tales in a modern context.

Fiction

Duey, Kathleen. *Amelina Carrett: Bayou Grand Coeur, Louisiana, 1863.* New York: Aladdin Paperbacks, 1999. This novel set during the Civil War takes place in a Cajun community. Amelina, the book's heroine, faces many challenges when Yankees hide in her home.

Holt, Kimberly Willis. *Mister and Me.* New York: Putnam Publishing Group, 1998. This novel is about an African American family living in a small Louisiana mill town. A headstrong young girl learns to accept her mother's new husband, Leroy.

Shaik, Fatima. *Melitte.* New York: Puffin, 1999. Set in Louisiana between 1765 and 1772, when the Louisiana colony was changing from French to Spanish hands, this novel follows Melitte, a young slave girl, and the changes that affect her and her family.

Wallace, Bill. *Blackwater Swamp.* New York: Minstrel Books, 1995. This lively mystery adventure is set in a small bayou town. Two boys solve a rash of burglaries with the help of a mysterious old woman they think is a witch.

WEBSITES

Info Louisiana

<http://www.state.la.us>

This state homepage provides information on Louisiana government, news, and education, among other topics.

Louisiana Travel—Welcome

<http://www.louisianatravel.com>

Find out about Louisiana's culture and tourism on the official Department of Tourism website.

Encyclopedia of Cajun Culture

<http://www.cajunculture.com>

From Acadia to Tabasco to Zydeco music, this site provides information about Louisiana's Cajun heritage, personalities, and places.

New Orleans Times-Picaynne

<http://www.neworleans.net>

Learn about national and Louisiana news in one of the largest newspapers in the state.

The houses and docks of Grand Bayou, Louisiana, sit right in the wetlands.

PRONUNCIATION GUIDE

Atchafalaya (uh-chaf-uh-LY-uh)

Baton Rouge (BAT-uhn ROOZH)

Caddo (KAD-oh)

Cajun (KAY-juhn)

Chitimacha (chihd-uh-MAH-shuh)

Creole (KREE-ohl)

Lafayette (laf-ee-EHT)

La Salle, René-Robert Cavelier, Sieur de (luh SAL, ruh-NAY-roh-BEHR ka-vuhl-YAY, SYER duh)

Mardi Gras (MAHR-dee GRAH)

Natchez (NACH-ehz)

New Orleans (NOO AWR-luhnz)

Ouachita (WAHSH-uh-taw)

Pontchartrain (PAHN-chuhr-trayn)

Shreveport (SHREEV-pohrt)

GLOSSARY

bayou: a marshy or very slow-moving body of water

Cajun: a person whose French-speaking ancestors came to Louisiana from Acadia in the 1750s. Acadia covered parts of eastern Canada and Maine.

civil rights movement: a movement to gain equal rights, or freedoms, for all citizens—regardless of race, religion, or sex

colony: a territory ruled by a country some distance away

Creole: a person whose ancestors came to Louisiana from France or Spain. Creoles also include people who have a heritage of French or Spanish and African roots.

immigrant: a person who moves into a foreign country and settles there

levee: a wall built along a riverbank to prevent the river from flooding. Levees are usually made by piling up sandbags and dirt.

Reconstruction: the period from 1865 to 1877 during which the U.S. government brought the Southern states back into the Union after the Civil War. Before rejoining the Union, a Southern state had to pass a law allowing black men to vote. Places destroyed in the war were rebuilt and industries were developed.

sediment: solid materials—such as soil, sand, and minerals—that are carried into a body of water by wind, ice, or running water

wetland: swamp, marsh, or other low, wet areas that often border a river, lake, or ocean. Wetlands support many different kinds of plants and animals.

INDEX

PHOTO ACKNOWLEDGMENTS

Digital Cartographics, pp. 1, 8, 9, 48; Franz-Marc Frei/CORBIS, pp. 2–3; Robert Holmes/CORBIS, p. 3, 45 (bottom); Joel Satore/www.joelsartore.com, pp. 4 (detail), 7 (detail), 18 (detail), 41 (detail, left), 43, 53 (detail, left); © Dick Dietrich, pp. 6, 39, 49, 75; Dianne Lindstedt, Louisiana Geological Society, LSU, p. 10; David Kelley, p. 11; Frederica Georgia, pp. 12, 15, 26, 40, 46, 47, 52, 60; Lynda Richards, pp. 13, 29, 44, 55; Kay Shaw Photography, pp. 14, 42; © Karlene Schwartz, pp. 16, 73; The Historic New Orleans Collection, Museum/Research Center, p. 19 (acc. #1980.205.35), 21 (acc. # 1970.1), 28 (acc. #1951.72); Historic Urban Plans, Library of Congress, p. 23; Independent Picture Service, pp. 25, 68 (second from bottom), 69 (second from bottom); Photograph Collection, Louisiana Division, New Orleans Public Library, pp. 27, 33, 35, 37; Leib Image Archives, p. 30; LSU-Shreveport Archives, pp. 32, 34, 36; Charles F. Swenson, p. 38; Thomas Ritter/Monroe-West Monroe Convention & Visitors Bureau, p. 41; Philip Gould/CORBIS, pp. 45 (top), 80; Diane Cooper, pp. 50 (left), 53 (right); © James Blank/Root Resources, p. 50 (right); Gary Peterson, Coastal Ecology Laboratory, LSU, p. 54; Coastal Restoration Division, Louisiana DNR, pp. 58, 59; George Karn, p. 61; Tim Seeley, p. 63, 71 (top), 72; TV Times, p. 66 (top); Pittsburgh Steelers, p. 66 (second from top); © Nancy Crampton, p. 66 (second from bottom); Hollywood Book & Poster Co., pp. 66 (bottom), 67 (top); New York Yankees, p. 67 (second from top); Collection of Thomas N. Whitehead, p. 67 (second from bottom); © Bettman/CORBIS, p. 67 (bottom); Kathryn Clay Gaiennie, p. 68 (top); © CinemaPhotos/CORBIS, p. 68 (second from top); Louisiana State Library, Louisiana Section, p. 68 (bottom); National Baseball Library, Cooperstown, NY, p. 69 (top); U.S. Mission to the United States, p. 69 (second from top); © CORBIS, p. 69 (bottom); Chuck Cook.

Front Cover (left), spine and back cover: © W. Cody/CORBIS;
Front Cover (right): © Owen Franken/CORBIS.